the wash of hours

Jason Conway

the wash of hours

Jason Conway

Black Eyes Publishing UK

the wash of hours
© Jason Conway 2025

First published in 2025
Black Eyes Publishing UK
Gloucester
United Kingdom

www.blackeyespublishinguk.co.uk

ISBN: 978-1-913195-32-8

Jason Conway has asserted his moral right under the Copyright, Designs and Patents Act, 1988, to be identified as the author of this work. All Rights reserved. No part of this publication may be reproduced, copied, stored in a retrieval system, or transmitted, in any form or by any means, without the prior written consent of the copyright holder, nor be otherwise circulated in any form of binding or cover other than that in which it is published and without a similar condition being imposed on the subsequent purchaser.

No part of this book may be used or reproduced in any manner for the purpose of training artificial intelligence technologies or systems. In accordance with Article 4(3) of the Digital Single Market Directive 2019/790, the author and publisher expressly reserve this work from the text and data mining exception.

A CIP catalogue record for this title is available from the British Library.

Edited by: Josephine Lay

Cover Design: Jason Conway, The Daydream Academy
                 www.thedaydreamacademy.com

Dedicated to Dad

Peter Conway 01/02/1937-09/02/2024

Your chandelier character illuminated my world

"It's a braw bricht moonlicht nicht the nicht."

(It's a beautiful, bright, moonlit night tonight.)

This Scottish saying is something my father often said when playing the fool. Its meaning has a poetic and linguistic power that reminds us to seek the light in darkness. The Conway family tree has Celtic origins.

Contents

11   j is my nickname & my character is low – a case for father

13   May you fester like father when he left Ward 122

14   I've read that it's good to spend time on a beach and be alone with your thoughts

15   Sestina as the storm

17   Almost lost in Porthcawl

18   I am the loving son

19   Restricted

20   It's only a matter of time

21   Oakwise

23   Bone Song

25   Take these joints of meat that writers feast upon

26   The urine infection made him see an angel

27   13

28   I want to scream at the sky

29   I find it hard to write about flowers

30   I have breath that draws like water

31   Chiaroscuro

32   Sixes and sevens

34   There is mist over Slad Valley

35   There's mist outside Bradwell Hall

36   How I used ekphrastic poetry to interpret my parents' marriage

38   Mother & Me & IWD

39   We shared a mirror

40   Don't Let My Brother Leave

41   I look to the valley

42	I lost control when I saw my brother at his lowest point
43	A Seaside Fantasy
45	*Only Fools and Horses* work
46	The collector of shadows
47	My mum tells me she has cancer
49	Micro poem mantra for self-help down the M6 to M5
50	In Jeopardy and lost for words
51	After swimming in the Lido, Father, I thought of you leaving
52	What my father said whilst delirious from a urine infection aged 85
53	My words are like bombs
54	My special ability to combat a high sensitivity to noise
56	The memory of rain in coastal Spain
57	What the doctor said
59	Emotional Contagion
60	It couldn't happen in a nursing home
61	Pigeon poetry
62	A swim that left me gasping
63	the wash of hours
65	An initial observer longs for natural motion
71	Acknowledgements
73	Jason Conway
75	Full Quotes

j is my nickname & my character is low – a case for father

I will be strong – an anchor made of mud that will let you slip straight into a chest & burn cold, then be a treasure sailing on a mantlepiece, unheard but loud, unseen but vivid. When that time comes, I'll have no arms to stop you, as I'll be water or the ghost of it – lung solid – a fish breathing grief, wishing to drown this dead sea with salt.

May you fester like father when he left Ward 122

Fuck your hospital wards — scrap them — go choke on Hippocratic truth
In urgency, my father cried — *God, help me* — a face of agony and salt
May you fester in bedsores — like father — when he left Ward 122

No sign of help from carers — neglected — no time for wounds to soothe
Beached on a rubbing bed — he floundered — no check-ups finding faults
Fuck your broken promises — accept them — go choke on Hippocratic truth

Our family knew no problem — his plight — no fire, no smoke, no whiff
Well treated, we assumed — good staff — chocolate boxes were bought
May you fester in bedsores — like father — when he left Ward 122

He struggled to survive — unhealed — he stewed in sweat and filth
In revelation, we cried — *he's broken* — for his integrity we fought
Fuck your doctored reports — show them — go choke on Hippocratic truth

Pumped with pain relievers — he believed — no need for change or bath
To us it's called abuse — no excuses — frail body tossed and mauled
May you fester in bedsores — like father — when he left Ward 122

The nursing home discovered — his infection — photo evidence for proof
The NHS may try to pardon — his abandon — but lessons must be taught
Fuck your sinking ship — scupper it — go sink in Hippocratic truth
May you fester in bedsores — like father — when he left Ward 122

I've read that it's good to spend time on a beach and be alone with your thoughts

to play with sand and shell, hear the roll of waves, the hiss of salted spray and a breeze that whispers

the feel of sun on exposed skin as I bury feet for comfort or the chill of coastal water that makes life so immediate

like a shark smelling blood and its single focal point to the presence of loss or the opportunity to embrace it.

To drift without weight or purpose in tidal forces; my back on rippled glass as I gaze at the infinite blue

with a disc of white that glows in the sky, that would bleach all vision if I stared into its empty eye.

My thoughts used to flow in abundance, in a mind without burden or pain as I melted into the sea's scape

to dream beyond the horizon of futures without limits. As I float here, above sand, my thoughts are now pebbles

that spill from my pores and press me to an airless ground, under the sting of waves that salt my eyes

from a clear view across the aquamarine glaze, to that line of endless light beyond reach. But I submerge myself:

with parents drowning by age, afraid of passing shadows that must sink when they cannot stay afloat

a brother in the depths of his internal ocean and the crush of its depression. And how numb I now feel

as a fish unable to swim, where no amount of courage or strength can lift me from this lightless place

under a pressure I cannot fathom, and the expanse of grief beyond that I must endure before the shore.

Sestina as the storm

Outside the window was a fierce storm;
the wind shouted and the hedge shook.
Decapitated teasels spiked the ground
as a weathered windmill was blurred.
A white dog and his man walked a field.
Jackdaws hovered as dark as the clouds.

Layers of burden blackened the clouds
as four birches stood naked in the storm
by swings that swung empty in the field.
Branches were broken, leaves shook.
Treelines, in the distance, were blurred
as beaks stabbed at things in the ground.

Compost bags flapped on the ground
while magpies played chess below clouds
and dogs barked behind gates, coats blurred.
Buildings and land were bruised by the storm
and people, on the news: distraught, shaken,
as green bladed grass thrashed in the field.

The flash of litter disturbed the field
as savage weather beat the ground:
cows blotted a hillside, colours shaken,
hilltops were scuffed by swollen clouds
and life felt urgent in the clutch of the storm,
while the wind clawed and the sky blurred.

A fir tree shivered, its needles blurred
while wood pigeons flurried from the field
as the washing line whipped in the storm.
Overturned pots broke on the ground
as the sun burnt a hole in the clouds.
Whatever bore those gusts, shook;

Walls were questioned, fences shook,
the garden smudged, borders blurred.
Remember feeling lost in the clouds?

When they called, who blinked out the field,
as the kettle howled and coffee was ground –
left us bitter, like the storm?

But the ground blurred and the room clouded.
Away from the field – rain expected – I shook
my head – caught the storm in my hands.

Almost lost in Porthcawl

I brave the chill of a growling Irish Sea for a wild swim.
It feeds on strength as I fight through hungry waves
that claw me down and out. Each desperate stroke
is a strain, as cold and fatigue seep into bones.
I see a vision of slipping below. My last breath
sucks in saltwater. My sight, a blur to blackness,
to nothing but a lost swimmer, claimed by a hunting sea
that spied a straggler; chased it to exhaustion.

But I kick and push, as much as my heart can give,
ignoring all the thoughts: of the tears of those I love,
the funeral and wake, my ashes cast beyond the coast.
That is my dying wish, as I came from a sea inside
a mother. She fears for my father, who will soon descend.
Would he grasp why I was taken before him?

I'm a child, paddling next to him in Rhyl. I'm splashed
and cry, as my eyes sting, till he rescues me, his little fish.
But I'm dragged back here, mauled by a wave that floods
my mouth. I swallow in panic, thrash, then choke it out.

In a thought: I worry whether the food waste is out,
as nothing should be wasted. I'd not be here, in this
ceaseless gut, as acid and my lunch rise in my throat,
will I get my IBS resolved and embrace more swims,
find out what unsettles me and be strong enough to grieve?

I beg for air, to reach the feel of sand under my feet,
where my legs can stride and lungs devour the sky.
Bring its heat with the joy of sanctuary on the shore.
For a moment, I am lost and helpless, waiting
for the end of me by a beast that feeds on breath,
drains the warmth from skin and beat from heart.

And yet, I survive, in this unpredictable world
full of pain and love, that sometimes suffocates.

I am the loving son

    that dotes on Mum and Dad.
I'm glad to help lift old-age burdens.
I'm here for them. I'm strong, loaded
with responsibility as I sort stuff out,
make great cups of tea, can tidy, dust and shift
with elbow polish as my armour shines.

Dad's left home for a nursing one,
gone from mum and she's alone.
It's a double blow and I'm a cushion.
I go when needed, help when needed,
listen when needed, and they call, daily.
I book Mum's taxis and search the internet

Can you order this? Can you take it back?

They wind me up in a string of asks.

*Let me get a pen. Yes, Mum, yes Dad, of course, I can.
Okay, don't worry, leave it to me.*

I solve problems, can fix things, be depended on
but there is tension and I can't hold on.
I am the loving son, about to be

undone.

Restricted

Yesterday, I hurt my back. I'm in constant pain, unable to walk without supportive reassurance; the surfaces that take my gargantuan weight as I slowly creep towards the kitchen sink for a drink of water or to make coffee for the fatigue I endure, & the lack of sleep. Two days ago, I was able to walk unaided & leave this house-trap, once my cosy space, that's expanded into a gothic mansion too arduous to navigate & laden with gloom. Each step is strained in a landscape of made things that seem to take an age to reach. Time is stretched beyond my patience & each moment & surface is observed, as there are few distractions here, other than the sharp stabs that snap me into focus or the birdsong outside an open window & passing cars on the road that I cannot cross or people chatting as they pass. I'm trapped & vulnerable here, facing the next few days in recovery, to build strength & find new ways to avoid the boredom overwhelming me. But I know I'll get better, as it's just a temporary injury & not what you have, Dad, confined in a nursing home or that wheelchair to move around all the homes within a home for the people left to wait for death, while I wait to leave & hope you won't.

It's only a matter of time

Your time matters to me, only, it will end too soon, but my time
will matter when I remember your time with me. What manner

of things will fill the times, when only I see you, behind my eyes,
time & time again & what mattered before, does not matter now,

only the times I am here with you at your bedside, holding your
hand, when only you cry & I can't. If only I could share these times

as tears, as you matter so much, to me, & all of it will have mattered
when your time is up & it's time for moving on & time to grieve –

to let all of this out – when its time. But there is no time for any
of that now & when I have to leave you, each time I come to visit, I

know its love that matters & saving all the times we had, for the times
I will feel them dry on my skin, & it's okay that I can only save time,

for now, as every moment left matters, to you and to me, only, I
can't show it to anyone, yet. But, I know, it's only a matter of time.

Oakwise
After Kevin Young

your years ring
        through my ears
bring sun to eyes—

unravel & blossom
        to seed smiles
on our faces

that hide
        today, tomorrow.
You weep

unable to see
        your future—
shed the rains

& soak bedding—
        drink the day
to sigh the night.

Your body—
        a thing of knots—
fingers gnarled

but tender
        & here, Father
I see you—

cut down—
        but I know
when you fall—

you'll live in me—
        your memory
as leaves

in this wind
        that shakes me
down— cold—

that will settle
        one day & warm
my ground

& soon, I'll know
        to say *goodbye*
in your room

in a forest of rooms.

Bone Song

I rise,
longing for the thaw,
in need of love.
I wait here petrified;
block the sun;
I wallow.

What light can come?
What good will come of this,
a winter mist?

I am numb;
into the abyss
all is drained from me:

the grief,
the chilled sweat
infects my sleep.

The Frightbringer
brings labour to my sighs.
No more smiles.

There are no more tears.

No more smiles
bring labour to my sighs.
The Frightbringer

infects my sleep:
the chilled sweat,
the grief.

All is drained from me.
Into the abyss,
I am numb;

A winter mist.
What good will come of this?
What light can come?

I wallow;
Block the sun.
I wait here petrified

in need of love.
Longing for the thaw,
I rise.

Take these joints of meat that writers feast upon

& throw them in the poet's pot
let their hunger stew the bones
& taste their poetry

The urine infection made him see an angel

My dad, dumbstruck, spoke in tongues;
Peter the infidel, blinded by faith.

In a hospital ward, a disciple prospected.
George crossed from bed to bed,
Searched for fever in the afflicted.
He sifted sentiment, exposed hope.

As morphine induced dad's euphoria,
Promises were dangled in delirium
Like crack spoons for dragon quests;
A champagne toast to the afterlife.

As George charged a fuming beast,
Peter, the atheist, scaled a bible.
With blade drawn, father surrendered
To a platinum tongue.

Death did not go hunting that day
But a preacher preyed.

13

Mum told me the story of why my father stopped going outside through Agoraphobia. I was a baby when it happened/he had his dream job as manager of a television store in Newcastle-Under-Lyme, or *'Castle'*, as we like to call it/he excelled as a master salesman, the king of his realm, and people swooped by to snatch the latest set, sold on fantasy/responsibility escapes from busy lives. Peter was forced to resign when Mother left me in his storeroom to work an extra shift at the local library where she cleaned to help with bills/but the burden couldn't be swept up. The book was thrown/Dad went home and lost twice: his salary and outdoor life. They worked hard as a couple but family life was priceless. He retreated indoors/couldn't leave home alone/made my teenage brother shield him on short-lived battles with shops or the mare of a town ride. I imagined a tale of how a dragon had cursed the air/made dad's home his dungeon/punished for the want of riches to spoil his wife and two sons. I discovered the truth of his sacking as mum reminisced in a café over cake/and I snorted coffee at the news. Dads in a nursing home/the beast has flown back/this time the fear is infectious and it won't leave without a sacrifice. All I can do is store his treasure in my sag of a chest as I wish I could fly away from all of this.

I've always preferred stories with happy endings but the doctor's best guess is weeks, if months, to live.

I want to scream at the sky

ask it why the world is so fucked up, to fuckity-fuck, as lucks a myth, a distant shine-less star smothered in shittery shite, and I'm not alright. I'm angry. Scratch that. I'm molten-animalistic-smokestack-white-hot-gunshot angry as life isn't fair and my dad's had his fairground scare of it: Arthritis, Osteoporosis, heart attacks, prostate cancer, urine infections, wheelchair bound, bed bound and destination terminal, so fuck it all and then some. I want to tear things up, rage a ruck, suck and swallow gallons of gin till I'm numb enough to sleep, cause my eyes can't weep for him, yet. I drink to forget. Keep your fucking promises of NHS care. Where the fuck was that when he needed it, prayed for it, the atheist-read-a-bible-begged-for it? He was stuffed with meds while you neglected open wounds, but don't worry he'll be gone soon. Shit, bloody effing fits, give me a break from it all, just for a bit, as sleeps a trial, sometimes. I'm hit hard in a juggernaut-screen-shatter-on-a-rain-filled nightmare of the lacerate-blood-sport-nail-wrench-slasher-film sort. There's no white or black, just a grey dreary-fucking-greydom-sun-swallowed teardom, a black-hole-hell-suck-me-whole-cell-by-cell-through final season in a relentless woe-book full of fuckery-fish-guts-piss-and-fag-buts clusterfuck. I suffer in unbuffered, unfiltered cliff-jump-to-nail-bed-impale-the-king-let-it-fucking-bring agony as life stings, makes it real, in my pick-my-skin-till-it-bleeds feel to feed my distractions, come cravings – the bright lights-Ferris-wheel-on-fire-torch-my-eyes actions. I'm tired, tired of it all and the world can go fuck itself, but it won't fix me as I'm broken, and it's time I spoke up. So, no more mother's-love-him-butter-never-melts-home-baked-smells-everythings-swell man. This half-filled glass peddler has to quit the optimistic bullshit and summon thunder. Why-oh-bastard-boiled why should dad suffer so much? What the fuck-fuck-fatalistic-fuck of an end for him, and I don't want to look up and see your sympathetic-rabbit-in-a-headlight-it'll-be-alright-Disney-movie stupid smiles. Plot spoiler. He's dying and that's the end of it. He's infected in his heart and this is my death-metal-serenade-with-cyanide-cherries-sick-of-your-pathetic-sighs-no-happy-ending-the-worlds-fucked-then-we-die outcry.

So forgive me, while I scream at the fucking sky.

I find it hard to write about flowers

because they seem perfect & life isn't
It's not always beguiling like lovers
letters about how life's so pleasant
& hey look at me I'm a shiny turd
that smells of dog rose & I'm a saint
& so bloody happy I can admire birds
on warm days & warm rain & resplendent
love all around & you could simply burst
with all your fucking smugness like pollen
burdens bees & makes my asthma worse
& I hope that you choke on that golden
dust as poets should be beautifully cursed
by thorns that prick us when written.

I have breath that draws like water

I don't feel pain – even when I pinch –
nothing is the same – I feel nothing.
I bite my teeth to stop tears – leaving
but they do not come – not yet – just
heat & the sting like ash in eyes.
I smile to others but it is just an action –
muscle memory, from before you went
just like all the will in my well. Sleep
is an obstacle to endure – dreams
that fall to fire where I am lost or drown –
say goodbye to you but the words don't
come – words the day can't speak –
boulders in my stomach.
Fingers press on closed eyelids – eyes
that don't want to see this world
without you – where there is no us.
I have dark circles that try to make me
disappear. Please let me go away from here
& all of this until my pain can find its way out.
These eyes are the cold of night that keep
me sedated – it is better this way – no need
to feel as feeling is accepting that you won't
cast a shadow under the sun – this sun
that is too real – makes everything real.
Please, universe, keep me curled in
the black. I want the dark of dark places
where nothing exists – needs me,
where thoughts can slow – slow
to moments – moments when
I can see your face smile back at me.
But, for now, I avoid everything
as I wish to be nothing, till I'm
a thing that can weep.

Chiaroscuro

We had the first colour TV in our grove
Dad was the manager of a TV shop
& we had a new set each year
Until he got the shove

He got dobbed in for keeping me
In the storage room at work as a baby
While Mum did her shift at 'Rists'
To make ends meet

But I wanted for nothing
In a childhood of Paisley & kitsch.

I preferred black and white
All those old movies to get lost in
Between the static of arguments
As I tuned out

I filled my world with fantasy
& all those war flicks
As I ignored traded bombs
Over Bourbons & builder's tea.

Sixes and sevens

1.
I remember the start of infant school. I started late. Mother held me back till I was ready. On the first day, I couldn't let go of the railings at the school entrance. I wasn't ready but the headmistress smiled – said lots of nice things, & I let the blood back into my hands. It left me when I was front of class – an exhibit. I felt all granite but I'd cracked by three, sat at the back & lost in Doodleland. After the bell, my hands wouldn't let go of the railings, till a bag of sweets, from Mother, guided me home.

2.
Fifteen years to get to this. This shy attempt to ask her out. I'm on my bike, alongside her, asking her if she would… I ride away embarrassed, head down & watching the front tyre blur, hoping she'd forget & not share it like candy. My class loved sweets & the next day they had a bag full – Love Hearts with 'Jason fancies Susan' on them, but they didn't dissolve – stuck on their tongues for the rest of the year.

3.
Did anyone enjoy being twenty-one? I didn't. The newspaper mention, the families' unwanted attention & the funeral party where I mourned my youth till the sherry trifle & the cheque from Dad arrived. My fresher's year is done & it's Summer & the money buys tickets to a 'mates away' in Greece. I taste a seven-day romance – watermelon sweet & I'm loving the skin & eyes & lips attention, but she went South after we landed.

4.
It's 1999 & my first time in Ibiza with my knit of friends, & they were after sex – whatever they could get. But I just wanted to dance, disappear from the world & fly. Our heads got left behind, many times, as we haunted the raves in waves of light, & all was love, especially the rush. My parents have no idea of those induced escapes where I could paint worlds behind my eyes & be reborn in chemical resurrection over seven days and nights.

5.
I've moved to Burslem, the 'Mother Town', to live & work in a new hub for 'arty types', & found a new family of six friends. Six shared lives with six new business start-ups, in six flats facing derelict bottle kilns – our link to the ceramic past when this place was the centre of the map, & I get on regional telly – Midlands Today & make my folks proud, astounded I could have a career in art. This little bohemia with ghosts of success, dreaming, like me, of second chances.

6.
It's been four years in a family home with a five and fourteen-year-old, in a dream I live in. We are four corners that hold the weather away – always summer. I've almost forgotten my parents & their arguments. It is that good... It was that good but I woke up alone, a bodiless relic in an airless museum – a head deafened by history – eyes afraid of the sun & a mind afraid to sleep, & I'm a tragedy stuck on repeat that will love again, but not yet.

7.
My parents unwind each day & time is split by motorways – one hundred & one-mile trips, each way. The drives up are filled with anxiety & the downs, I'm on empty. I'm on call but I'm wired like a bad telephone exchange from Mum's expertise in quiet destruction & Dad's finite demands. I'm their TV & they fight over the remote in a weekly repeat. When this show ends, I'll be a scared child, again, in need of sweet thoughts to remind me of them – the home that I can't let go.

There's mist over Slad Valley

It rises over rolls of fields
as treetops bob like broccoli
in a soup that gently winds

under this winter cloudscape.
It flows over folded hillsides
like bed sheets being shaken.
9:30 am. Time for Dad's meds.

The news warns of minus seven
on my phone. The feed freezes
as my father calls to vent.
I wish for a pill for his disease.

His voice brings me warmth again.
Like this valley, I'm full of tears.

There's mist outside Bradwell Hall

so thick you could slice like icing.
Inside, I've got my tea, lukewarm
and thick porridge. Needs a knife.

I watch TV. A show about nature,
discussing the loss of peat beds.
My sheets need changing. *Nurse.*
It's 9:30 am. Time for my meds.

Minus seven. The news, this morning.
Pensioners struggle with heating;
the old and the Earth are losing,
like this disease has me beaten.

Worried, I call my son, start crying.
Both of our futures are uncertain.

How I used ekphrastic poetry to interpret my parents' marriage
(The iconic paintings: Tretchikoff's Chinese Girl and Lynch's Tina are a familiar memory of my childhood home in the Potteries, North Staffordshire.)

1.

The Chinese girl, with a green face & red lipstick,
looked away from us as she stood by her window,
above the fireplace shelf, littered with kitsch.

She was unfinished & uncomfortable & it showed –
like my mother, in her eternal drag of domesticity,
that he expected of a loving, loyal, seventies house-

wife & the irony of her part-time job as a library
cleaner, that I later understood was her escape
from the claustrophobia of our home & Dad's eyes

that saw the dust that I, their child, didn't notice
or care was wiped clean – like Mother's missing
tears that rarely expressed the hidden strain

of marriage – a country girl, bound in a brickscape
& this Chinese girl, wearing mother's frown.

2.

Tina looks out from her woodland window
& stares at my father, inviting him inside

her wilderness, full of desire, luring him away
from our family home of Mr & Mrs & two

sons, who wonder why their parent's argue
over the smallest things with conviction, till

all is ash – like the fireplace, heavy in our lungs
& the fag cloud that stains the Artex ceiling

but this other woman frames his temptation –
naked & unburdened in her sultry wilds –

like my mother's passion had once beckoned –
a rural lass who escaped to this town, away

from a strict childhood & as she slaves at home,
I'm too young to know if she regrets these years.

Mother & Me & IWD

An acronym for sisterhood; the power held
within; a vine that holds firm; as rope to sail
that caught the wind; the chaos of man
made good by magic; clay of goddess,
shaped tall as cedars, our feet given wings
to soar above shadows cast upon you.

Faithful as river flow, you are the source
of breath, thirst of ground, a meditation
of connection. As boys we tested banks,
raced & rested, understood that we are fluid.

Daughter, sister, mother; unbreakable
weave of woman, patriarchal bound,
you are wise, resilient & today, you rise.
Every day you rise to those dry as desert.
Sun to seeds, lift us high as cliffs over coast
to see beyond that which divides.

Wet from womb, we are born as stars to eyes
reflecting unconditional love. Sing us peace
as doves, make us boys again, teach us
to listen & witness the balance you bring.

Around islands, your tide is magnetic,
inevitable, unstoppable. Surge in symphony
your lunar rhythm, blend these gendered borders.
Mother Justice, we are blind by privilege.
We are not grand castles or reefs to repel.
In truth, we are equal as sand.

We shared a mirror

You taught me how, held my hand up
to my hairless face, covered in foam.
Just a child, I didn't understand the need
to hold up appearances for others.
I mimed your hand, watched bristles
litter the sink water as they dropped
& your mistakes were marked in red & I
saw that even adults made mistakes –
even Dad. I didn't know then, that men
wear masks – that Father's would fall
one day. I thought he was invulnerable
– my superhero dad with a shining face
that protected me from harm. You hid
your mistakes well – too well, I'd say,
& I learned to mirror you and made
my own masks & my own mistakes.
Some have healed but not all, as some
will stay locked deep inside, & I know
it's wrong, but Dad, you taught me how.

Don't let my brother leave

My big brother has just thrown me in the nettles
He's pinched me & stuck a raisin up my nose
I am told   he's said he's sorry
But I wish I was older

•

My brother skips school   He's stopped going
& he's at home without any qualifications
Though he teaches me lessons
I don't understand

•

My older brother isn't that big or strong anymore
& I can arm wrestle him & pin him down
Around town   he delivers flowers
Knows everyone's smile

•

My bloody brother has a steady girlfriend he's seeing
But he still lives at home with the folks
I'm off to Uni   yet he's cleverer
I can't wait to leave

•

My unshaven brother has seven children that he adores
He loves his chaos & telling the worst jokes
He's broke but rich in life
& I love them all

•

Your brother's left the house   says he wants to kill himself
He's got a drink problem   won't eat or ask for help
Two stone   he's lost   He's lost
My brother   all bones

I look to the valley

as it fades from view
        beyond the boundary.
The horizon mists —

comforts contours —
        the vales wisdom
released in white.

I forget the details,
        before this view
watered my eyes,

how the kiss of sun,
        eased the ground —
raised a memory.

I remember my father,
        wise & old, laid
on a sodden bed,

wishing for release.
        Of his conditions, I wish
he could become

the mist,
        have his outlines
relaxed, his tears

dispersed to sky,
        away from his valley —
a withered earth

deep in prayer.
        When the soil forgets,
he will be missed.

I lost control when I saw my brother at his lowest point

I'm a begrudging twin in a permanent house share and I can't abide him so I lock him in his room and he's only allowed out on his 'Sermon Sundays'   they are not Sundays   not always   just biblical brimstone days where he preaches lessons to the deserving so he says and puts the fear of any deity in them   I'm on a diet as I've cut down on red meat and only have the stomach for it on his days out   he's devout and dedicated and he rehearses in the dark oiling his words as he's all method   and god does he crave an audience like a fist needs a face   he worships the sun as an arsonist and you're the touchpaper   like a bear after winter he craves blood and I imagine he'd bathe in yours if he could   he's all chemical and I call him Caesium under my breath   and secretly I admire his fire but pray you never see him combust   he'd scald you when he spat his twisted scripture   and I'm not religious but I love the quiet when he's burnt himself out   when the house becomes a church and his pyrotechnic presence no longer troubles me   the trouble with being his twin is that you can hardly tell us apart

A seaside fantasy

Blondie's Sunday Girl
plays on the breeze and melts
sweetly in our ears
as we picnic on the beach —
become lost in each other.

We write messages
in bleached sand — sun hot — with toes
fingers, sticks and stones.
Our names get smudged by the tide
like our Sundae ice-cream smiles.

We laugh as we bite shell
blown in our sandwiches,
loose wrappers to wind,
brave those freezing waves and splash
each other — scream a chorus

that challenges the ears
of all that has ears nearby —
even dogs agree
this place cannot be quiet
when kids greet the Irish sea.

~~~

I loved those seven
summers spent in Aberystwyth,
losing coins in slots,
being chased by my brother
round a four-berth caravan.

If I close my eyes,
I can taste the brine, smell chips
drenched in vinegar —
wince with each swallow, feel grass
tickle bare feet, hear seagulls

argue overhead
like my parent's loose baggage;

their tongues like windsocks
duelling for the last, last word
as I chased you for kiss-chase.

I think of the pier,
it's endless amusements,
bandits with one arm
stealing sighs by the chest-load
as we shared candyfloss lips.

I lost you on that
unlucky-for-me year — my
Heavenless Seventh.
We made castles on the beach —
said we'd get married in one.

We stared across waves
as the water stole our dreams.
Mum and dad shouted,
again and scared you away —
made my eyes become the sea.

Only Fools and Horses work

and Dad, you had the gab, all wrapped up,
ready to sell to the hypnotised,
but you worked, so damn canine hard
to keep your knitted family cushty.

You've got a GCE in Art…when you gettin' a propa job?
You and mum certainly kept me grounded,
concrete boots for wandering feet until my
gown and mortar cemented the punchline.

This time next year Jay…we'll be millionaires,
you'd say to me; even now, when
there's no change in your meter
and the cold's well and truly set in.

Your chandelier character illuminated my world
until you got stuck in a dodgy dealing
that went Conference-shaped, and we crowded
round your hospital bed catching crystal tears.

You used to call me Rodney in jest but Dad,
I confess there's no Cassandra crossing
to greener grass for you. No more
grandad's sea tales to keep the kids anchored.

There's a burglar shadowing you from the inside,
no neon paint tracks for the docs to find.
Early signs undetected until a fair cop
reluctantly charged your life sentence.

This time next year…I won't be rich

but I'll have a million precious blinks
of a gifted workhorse that fooled around,
proud of my art career, take that, Rodney
and pukka memories that no-one can rob.

The collector of shadows

I feel a presence that pulls on my breath
each time my brother calls. I struggle for breath.

A sudden cold strength overpowers my chest
like his sounds have fists that punch my breath.

He is getting worse & he mithers too much –
can't let things go – a disturbance in breath.

His weight loss is a scare – he's barely with us
like you could knock him over with a breath.

I'm not going nuts – he says. Counselling refused.
A brother obsessed – those words in his breath.

Each fraught encounter – a reach of claws
that scratch out words as I wince for a breath.

I know it's not real but I imagine him possessed
& those panicked words are not from his breath.

I can recall – as winter haunted, he was himself.
A wife, kids, parents & me, warmed his breath.

Cursed by dark news, he'd no stomach for life.
Consumed by war in Ukraine – a chill to his breath.

As spring marched, I witnessed a wraith
that fed a premonition – an end to his breath.

He roams an addled mind, a collector of shadows.
The darkest: not eating, the attempt on his breath.

My brother broods in a space without walls
& chases death. All I can do is hold my breath.

My mum tells me she has cancer

My mum tells me she has cancer & she doesn't need a doctor to tell her & she's not as stupid as people think & she knows best   She's been suffering with dehydration for two months & she's spitting white froth & has diarrhea all the time & the surgery doesn't seem to want to help or think it's serious   She's been taking in samples for the hospital but they can't accept them as she's not done them correctly   She's been told to eat lots of small meals during the day & drink plenty of water but she says she keeps bloating when she drinks   She should be taking Paracetamol four times a day but doesn't like taking tablets   She tells me she's depressed & can't go on like this & no one is helping   She doesn't want to be left on her own in her home anymore full of stuff she doesn't need anymore & she's lost so much weight that she uses a peg by her waist to hold up her trousers   She'd be better off taking all the tablets & be done with it   I tell her that it's not fair   the doctors need to find out what's wrong before they can help & if she's lonely & depressed she can call the Wellbeing Centre down the road for wellbeing but she tells me she doesn't need seeing & there's only me that bothers with her anymore & no one is listening but I'm one hundred miles away & I'm struggling myself & I wish I could help & I wish I wasn't helpless & wish I could wish my way out.

∞

My family's collapsed as my brother's in a breakdown & father's in a nursing home & mother may have cancer & my mental health is suffering & my body is suffering & sometimes I feel empty & I don't want to meet friends & when I speak to my mum I feel numb like my heart's been cut out & all the feelings I should have have drained out   I've run out of the will to say things that could help as she doesn't seem to listen & keeps repeating everything negatively   It's not healthy for her to be this way   I can feel myself crawling into myself into the safe space where I shut the world out   wish it would all stop & fix itself but it won't & I'm trying my best but I know that time's running out & it all feels wrong   My parents don't have long but I wish I wasn't the only one that can help   I feel helpless & the only thing I can do is to listen to her telling me it'd be better if she was dead   my brother looks dead & father soon will be & I listen knowing that part of me feels dead   the part that should feel something   I don't tell her that I get cold lately & feel my body shutting down   When it does I have to lie down & sleep   Sometimes I wonder if I'll wake up & this was all a bad bad dream & I've found the feelings to put into words & scream & tears can be shed & some warmth is felt but it's not   I know there's worse to come & worse to be said & right now I envy the dead.

Micro poem mantra for self-help down the M6 to M5

Inhale...[hold]...
                release...
                              & repeat...

In *Jeopardy* and lost for words

(Jeopardy! Is an American television game show that features a quiz competition in which contestants are presented with clues in the form of answers, and must phrase their responses in the form of questions.)

Why use a single word when you can use so many – as many as you like, to describe the same thing and on multiple levels or add flesh to the bones to keep them warm – as close company keeps us attentive – like fog that can cleverly distract the reader from the ghost who is deafened by the silent notes, so hides until the last line and then stares at you, in your face and makes eye contact, so you can see it as clearly as a polished diamond in a river of words, after you've got your eyes dirty and panned the silt of every one of them but then decide to tear out the paper, scrunch it and toss it into the fire, till the poet sees the value of reduction as the letters disappear to leave the ash that is left and buried, buried for millennia, after millennia, on a prehistoric level, until, they've dug out the gem of a skeleton and laid it there, bare on the page for us to marvel at, on a flat museum – and so my point to all of this is... what should the reader be gaining when reading a poem, that is written using all of the infinite options that the English language has to offer, when also considered with the infinite applications of poetic technique available, or the absence of the number of precious carats that could dangle from lines in the road of meaning that comprise a successful resolution, if the poet is efficient and writing for the rider of a donkey to make their epic journey that much more profound, when they reach the quandary of the end point and the choices that are open in the space beyond that end – when the answer should be realised in a single, synapse firing moment – unfiltered and pure... and that is the final word, to all of the final, final words that could have been used to explain this concise example of the need for...

What is the question?

After swimming in the Lido, father, I thought of you leaving

Neurons fire in a white waving mesh on a light blue floor, as praying hands
search for the dry sun & glass is blown in amorphic sculptures which rise,
then vanish as if they never were, recalled in bubbles inside my mind.

Under the surface, all is muted & yet, in constant change: of pattern, shade,
movement & the dance of light, as spheres of breath ascend. Feet kick, hands
push, bodies glide & minds focus on the immediacy of motion from wall,

through water, to wall. Fingers & toes sense waters flow as hair undulates
to its cool stroke of silver rhythm & I rock like a baby in a weightless cradle,
as though sway is a meditation to regress to the womb of a world within

a world, where existence was simple & snug, with no pain, fear, cry or gasp
but this place is like the cycle of birth to death & all that is in between is flux.
Filled with the bond of air & heart & I wish for more time here to watch

our time that shifts before us. Soon, I will only remember you as a life
through many ripples, as my eyes pool & bring the memory of your presence
to my skin & I will wave to you through infinite waters.

What my father said whilst delirious from a urine infection aged 85

The	*Spanish*	*are coming*	
C	*O*	*R*	
Convict	*On*	*the Run*	
What if	*they block*	*the borders?*	

Unsteady	I tiptoe	over spent shells
shocked	by the impact	of broken cover

This civil war   is a minefield   needs a flagbearer

But Dad   *It's okay*   *we're safe*   *in England*

Ceasefire called	inquisition over	& peace brokered	
over a stream	of antibiotics	soft words	& weak tea

My words are like bombs

when they arrive so unexpectedly & cause the maximum damage
to my unsuspecting casualty, like a nail bomb – so neat,

concealed in a pretty red ribboned parcel with a note saying
You thought acupuncture was bad, but here's a surprise

that will have you in A&E wishing you'd done what I'd asked.
By the time you recover, you're riddled with scars

as my sunshine backside radiates melanoma while you send, *I don't wish I
was here* postcards from your fawn-like face. I'll obliterate them

in my blitzkrieg, as I rain in your ears & taunt you with sugar sounds that
won't soothe those singes. My medicine

language given to the bad boy that says no, who's off being bloody
independent. But I demand your time, as I'm the woman

that birthed you, son. Do what I say & you'll have mercy tomorrow.
But you failed today, so accept your surrender,

remember your mother feels joy when you're obedient; sends hellfire
when you disobey her. May you suffer

exquisitely, as eating chocolates laced with acid. Come close, bend your
piglet ear to your phone speaker & keep listening

Here's a kettle for your thoughts dear & I'll ram a throatful of sand soap, as
my demands are not accepted & how you'll blister

till I scrape you off my soles & speak with notes of love & understand
that this is the love of a mother betrayed by your excuses

as you're left decimated by kindness. But none of this is my voice;
this is what you imagine when you're not in my earshot

where you bolster your brain from words that arrive sweet & explode, as
saying *Sorry, I can't come* will be your Armageddon.

My special ability to combat a high sensitivity to noise

Are you like me? Have you ever felt like you weren't here
like me on this park bench, as in not present – nowhere – lost?
But not to say that you're worried or disturbed by this
transcendental meditation beyond people and place
And you have no urgency to reappear or go *ARRGH*
to make people jump, to make sure of it
that you are present in their vicinity and not invisible
but haunting the space they inhabit

And that is not to say you don't exist
have vanished, aren't here or there, or anywhere
although you're an expert at blending in or blending out
like you can summon a reality eraser when you feel like lead
become the white space of an undrawn sketch.

Have you been in a busy room or a room with a few, or just a room
where you took one long deep cool breath like a free diver
let yourself fade out or darken into darkness
And you're not there, there is no room and you drift
all is quiet and still, or at least it has the noise you want and not theirs
unwelcome like thunder – that you writhe from like sharp sounds
of alarming news or tiny talk for awkward, anxious silences.

Are you like me? Often present but not present
like a shift in the light or a rainbow behind clouds
Do you dislike crowds as much as the smack of confrontation
or all those strained situations in need of attention and action, like
my parents who became emergency sirens through age and illness
And my shadow brother, scared of the sun and his thoughts
or friends I feel uneasy with, as I hear too much.

I like to be over there – in *my* there, wandering an Autumn Forest
stepping over the softness of the dead. I envy the rot, undisturbed
while I bathe in shimmers, submerge in that lucid lake, as nothing
      and everything all at once,
muffled by rusting mulch – where I deconstruct and consider my state,
or lack of it, like I'm a catalyst for petrichor
a dormant aerosol at rest in absence.

Not like all those walking, talking ones I know, full of hiss and stink
when thinking is impossible. So I leave without moving
all the awkward distractions that thump my ears,
while I wish I were deaf or an unturned stone, surrounded
by trees and leaves, left alone on this bench.
But no matter how good I am at disappearing,
some people are herons in a deluge, hungry for attention
And I'm forced to resurface.

The memory of rain in coastal Spain

Demerara dusted caramel sponge spread
with apple & blueberry jam with a sea
of frosted crests & finished with yellow
& red numbers that flicker as they catch
the light of a white blur floating in a slight
hue of the palest blue rippled room
with the faintest brush of iced clouds
that lined this sugarscaped delight
detailed with rice paper doily umbrellas
in pink, blue & orange over a sprinkling
of fondant shells on my fifty first birthday
as I drift on Andalucía's Costa De La Luz
away from the sweet bitter salt
of my father's dying candle.

What the doctor said

i
*Hello. Good morning. Please take a seat, while I get
your notes up. I will be taking a blood test, today.
You are dehydrated, so we need to take blood
tests to monitor how you are doing. It's nothing
serious, just routine tests. To help you get better,
eat small meals through the day. Salads are good
& plenty of greens. Try to avoid stodgy foods.
Take two paracetamol tablets, four times a day.
Feeling sick is a common symptom of dehydration.
Drink plenty of water to keep you hydrated.
At least three litres a day to help you recover,
& if, at any point, you start to feel worse,
come straight back in & let us know.*

Ii
*Mum, the doctor said you're dehydrated. That's
all the blood tests are for. You need to drink three
litres of water a day but more if you can. Just have
lots of mouthfuls, instead of glasses of water, to stop
you feeling sick & take two paracetamol, four times
a day. They may need to do more blood tests, mum,
to check how things are going. Have you got much
food in? What about salad & green veg?*

iii
*This is my son. He's come with me to listen to you,
as I'm a bit deaf & might miss something you say.
He can tell me what you said, when we get home,
as I won't remember it all.*

*Listen carefully to what the doctor says, & tell me
what I need to do when we're back home.*

*Yes, I had a bit of salad, yesterday. But, you know
how I like cheese. They're not telling me the truth,
you know. I'm not as stupid as they think & I'm sure
it's cancer, I've got. Why won't they tell me? I don't
like taking tablets, never have, & drinking water
makes me bloat & feel sick. Look at me, this is how
bloated I am. You tell me, why they haven't told me,*

*I've got cancer? I know I have. The doctors are useless.
Why won't they do something to help?*

Emotional Contagion

My brother says *What if the cordless phone breaks? What if the rechargeable batteries stop working? Can you get some extra ones, just in case?*

I say *It's okay, the clue is in the name and things usually go wrong in threes.*

My brother says *Come. Look, the phone's no good – the signal has no bars.*

I say *What? That's odd, just leave it for a few hours… look the bars have come back – just a random glitch.*

My brother says *What if the landline stops working and my mobile, and my spare mobile? What will I do? And what if you aren't around when that happens?*

I say *It's okay, you're more likely to win the lottery.*

My brother says *Can you go to town and check my bank account – in the hole-in-the-wall? What if I've no money? What if the machine eats my card? I don't need a statement.*

I say *It's okay, they're not that hungry…*

I say *You won't believe this, but it's been eaten. I put your card in and keyed in the pin, and the balance was positive. But the screen went black and said:*

SHUTTING DOWN… SYSTEM ERROR…

I think *What if negative emotions could infect machines…*

My brother says *What? What can we do? Will you call the bank for me? What if they don't answer? What if they're closed?*

I say *If only… Okay, all sorted – a new card is on its way – due in three days.*

My brother says *What if it gets lost in the post, the phones die and I can't call anyone?*

It couldn't happen in a nursing home

After eating, father wiped his face. A man at the home took offence
& began to shout at him to stop. It seemed odd they had gotten
so annoyed, they lost control. Dad gets angry, now he's older,
stuck in a wheelchair, pestered with bedsores that have stayed

since he moved from the hospital, in constant pain & looked so pale,
to a safe place where people care, encourage him to eat regular
meals & he looks much healthier, has the strength to wipe away
mess around his mouth & chin, which had been a challenge to him

when he didn't want to eat in a ward where he'd been mistreated,
allowed to suffer & wither, until the doctors transferred
him, to be nursed for end of life. He waved a butterknife
at his disturbed antagonist – threatened to stab them with it

if he didn't stop complaining about something, so *bloody crazy*.
The home had to make a report, after my Dad had been escorted
back to his room to calm down. I discovered this when I came to visit
him afterwards & the matron told me what had happened earlier

when she said she'd taken action, lodged an incident with the owners.
She explained it wasn't his fault, completely, but threatening to assault
a resident – even with a butterknife, or the confusion with the wiping,
that baffled the staff that morning, wasn't right & was *a bit naughty*.

She'd done *well to not giggle* at the two of them – so surreal,
fighting like a pair of toddlers. *Peter wouldn't have got far,
as he couldn't push his wheelchair*. Part of me wished I'd said
Well, I'm not surprised, as dad loves a good spread.

Pigeon poetry

It's a hot morning as I walk with my Rescue Hound
through a browning park & the streets of Stroud.
I reach the verge with a tarnished red bench & surprise
of ripe blackberries. I pick one – they're too early
this year – a taste so sharp I spit it out & wince.

Warm drips dapple the nape of my neck.
I look up to see two pigeons on a branch.

I wipe luck dry in this unprecedented July heat-
wave to acknowledge this timely avian metaphor
that exposes the irony of British reticence.
Since a child I have struggled with confrontation –
Mum & Dad's habitually traded insults.

The stain of their bad news lingers.
This dark fruit has left me sour.

A swim that left me gasping

As I slipped through the water's wind sculpted surface, submerged air
made its presence known and sought escape from a pressurized vessel
and when released into the flow as mirrored globes that raced for sky
and passed between the balance of two temperamental atmospheres, I
was dragged back to the sensitive boy that shouted in a tempest where
they didn't listen to my tidal surges that never reached the arms of the shore
left to roll and wane to an uneasy stillness under a loom of clouds
as rain hit the teeming paisley carpet, watched by yellow glass-blown fish
and dried with the dust of their wrecks as I dreamed of the day
away from the savagery of two waves that crash against each other
that deafened my cries for calm – a child at sea hoping for hypothermia
I sank through the pattern of pile into the deep wetness beyond
the squall and sting of spray, where I held my breath so many times
under turbulence and waited for my parents' love to ebb back.

The wash of hours

I walked from Kerne Bridge car park, where boats were launched
to where I crossed over the River Wye, went through a metal gate
into a field lined with Himalayan Balsam that flared its banks

along a narrow path like the infection in my father's bloodstream
that took root without a cure. If this wilderness were mind medicine
I had a dose that flooded relief to eyes with memories of pastimes.

Of timeless meanders with parents; a child in overflow in the wash
of hours. And on this day, I drifted, made a blackberry tongue,
channels through grass, pebbled legs from nettle stings as I passed

and water whispered round shingle, of its inevitable flow beyond
these soothing moments that carried life into the distant silence.

I thought of how your current slowed each day, of how it would end,
how this heat was made bearable, ahead of a season of shedding.

An initial observer longs for natural motion

Bless the unseen vista
Beyond this smoke

Bless the southern wind
To melt this frost

Bless the distant rain
To salt this ground

Bless the river
To breach this dam

Bless this dry leaf
That clings to water's edge

Bless the day I hear you say
Let go

"Give sorrow words; the grief that does not speak whispers the o'er-fraught heart and bids it break."

— **William Shakespeare**

"And once the storm is over, you won't remember how you made it through, how you managed to survive. You won't even be sure, whether the storm is really over. But one thing is certain. When you come out of the storm, you won't be the same person who walked in. That's what this storm's all about."

— **Haruki Murakami, Kafka on the Shore**

"When it is darkest, we can see the stars."

— **Ralph Waldo Emerson**

'Chinese Girl'
Vladimir Tretchikoff

'Tina'
J.H. Lynch

These two paintings are referenced in the poem on page 36.

Acknowledgements

My heartfelt thanks go to all involved in making this book happen.

Firstly, to my late father, to whom this book is dedicated, for teaching me to embrace humour in the darkest times. I will always cherish reading '*Only Fools and Horses* work' to him and my mother in his room at the care home, and later at his funeral.

Thank you to Josephine and Peter Lay of Black Eyes Publishing UK for trusting me with my work, for Josephine's excellent editing skills, and making this book a reality. I'd also like to thank professors Tim Liardet, for his laser insight, and Lucy English, my manuscript tutor, whose guidance helped to shape the manuscript, in its first incarnation, during my Master's Degree at Bath Spa University. Additional thanks go to Adam Horowitz and JLM Morton for their invaluable feedback.

My final thanks go to my partner, Michelle, whose love and support has kept me nourished through difficult times, and my daughter Eva and Stepdaughter Georgina, who constantly remind me that life is for living, laughing, learning and loving, as if each day was a dance like no one's watching!

Jason Conway

Photo: Angela Fitch Photography

Jason Conway is a professional daydreamer, director of the Gloucestershire Poetry Society and editor of award-winning art and literary magazine Steel Jackdaw. His poetry has been published in The Blue Nib, Poetry Bus, The Poetry Village, Impspired, Wildfire Words, Dreich, Fevers of the Mind, Ink Sweat and Tears, The Phare. And, in numerous anthologies – including New Generation Beats Anthology 2024, broadcast on BBC Sounds, and selected for The John Muir Trust's Wild Moments. Jason has performed at at the 2000 Trees Festival and read at Cheltenham Poetry Festival. He has an MA in Creative Writing from Bath Spa University, and is an Arts Council funded poet. Jason was commissioned by the ADHD Foundation for the Stoke on Trent Neurodiversity Umbrella Project (2022). His commissioned poem is on permanent display in Hanley's peace garden, along with a word art mural in collaboration with We Are Culla (2023). He was the inaugural judge for Gloucestershire Wildlife Trust Poetry Competition 2023. Jason has facilitated workshops in schools, for The Space In-between Festival, Gloucestershire Libraries, Stroud District Council, and Gloucestershire Writers' Network. He was a member of the Word Space 2024-25 cohort – a 12-month development programme by Literature Works for South West writers. When Jason isn't being creative, he enjoys escaping into nature, cold water swimming, making healthy homemade food, sci-fi and fantasy, living an authentic autistic life and admiring his stone collection.

Full Quotes

"Jason Conway's collection is heartbreakingly exquisite, with his ingenious use of nature's healing yet destructive powers to reflect the co-existing nature of love and pain; undeniable beauty and inevitable change. Authenticity shines through in this poetic exploration of life and loss. He expresses the toughest realities tenderly with seamless, compelling storytelling."

– Jemima Hughes

'*the wash of hours* by Jason Conway is a poignant and deeply personal collection of poetry that navigates themes of grief, memory, and familial bonds with stunning emotional intensity. Conway's use of striking imagery, lyrical phrasing and bold experiments with form immerses the reader in moments of loss and reflection, particularly in the face of a father's decline and a son's struggles. This collection lingers in the mind, offering a powerful meditation on time, loss, and the quiet beauty found in life's fleeting moments.'

– JLM Morton

Jason Conway's *the wash of hours* is a deeply affecting collection of poems navigating a complicated landscape of caretaking for loved ones while struggling not to neglect one's own essential care. Brave, poignant and important work.

– John Burroughs, 2022-23 U.S. Beat Poet Laureate

A wonderfully crafted collection of personal poetry that has you enwrapped in the turmoil of life's struggles. Some very difficult subjects are handled with aplomb, and you share the anger and unfairness of such things. There are some deft touches too, in which you are reminded that Jason is a first-class writer who can make you feel every emotion, be that in the pit of your stomach or the flutter of the heart. An absolutely stunning read.

– Nick Degg – Stoke-on-Trent Centenary Poet Laureate

Like a tidal echo, memory and memorial wash through Jason Conway's debut collection in little eddies and vast waves. These are salt-sprayed and potent poems of tenderness and rage, numbness and hope. There is much to discover beneath their surfaces.

– Adam Horovitz, poet, performer and editor.

Jason Conway's debut collection *'the wash of hours'* charts the difficult territory of caring for elderly parents 'drowning by age'. His father's decline impacts the entire family. His mother becomes needy and faces a possible cancer diagnosis and his brother falls into depression. Facing all this the narrator is portrayed like a child overwhelmed by the power and terror of the sea. 'What light can come?' he asks.

We feel the pain of a son trying to shore up a disintegrating family and his awareness of the limitations of his sensitivity. 'I wish I were deaf or an unturned stone, surrounded by trees and leaves.' Swimming and drowning are strong themes here but there is also a delicate observation of the natural world; rain in coastal Spain is remembered as 'Demerara dusted caramel sponge spread with apple & blueberry jam with a sea of frosted crests.'

Conway experiments with form and approach. Some of the poems read like prose or disjointed memories. He displays a quiet deadpan humour which lifts this dark story out of melodrama. Titles like 'What my father said while delirious from a urine infection' and the ridiculousness of medical speak in 'What the Doctor Said' give the whole collection a breathing space in mood.

The final poem, the title one, ends in a moment of reflection that all this pain will gradually shift like a stifling hot summer does 'in a season of shedding'.

– Dr Lucy English – Professor of Creative Enterprise and The Spoken Word. Co-director of Lyra, Bristol Poetry Festival

www.ingramcontent.com/pod-product-compliance
Lightning Source LLC
Chambersburg PA
CBHW072105110526
44590CB00018B/3327